Cheetah
CONSERVATION

Written by Susan Brocker

The author and publisher would like to thank Cheetah Outreach for their help with this book.

CONTENTS

THE RACE TO SURVIVE

Racing through the tall, waving grass, the spotted form is a blur of speed. Before the zebra even knows danger is near, the chase is on. The spotted cat springs through the air and knocks the zebra off its feet. Within a moment, the female cat suffocates its prey, and then calls to its cubs to join the feast. The cats eat their kill quickly, alert and wary of larger, stronger *predators* that pose a danger. These cats are cheetahs – nature's most graceful hunters.

These cheetahs are on the lookout for both predators and prey.

"Cheetah" is a Hindi word that means "spotted one." This species of cat is one of the oldest on Earth. Cheetahs have been around for about four million years. Today, they are found only in parts of Africa and a few areas of Asia (see map on page 6). Once, however, they roamed four continents, including an area of North America that is now the states of Wyoming, Texas, and Nevada. Cheetahs disappeared from that area, and from Europe, at the end of the last Ice Age, almost 10,000 years ago.

Unfortunately, these long-surviving animals are now facing their greatest danger. As humans continue to move into their territory, cheetahs are being forced closer and closer to *extinction*. Loss of *habitat*, *poaching*, competition from large predators such as lions, and trapping and shooting by farmers are killing off the wild cheetah. In 1900, there were nearly 100,000 cheetahs. Today there are only about 12,500, and nearly ten percent of these live in *captivity*.

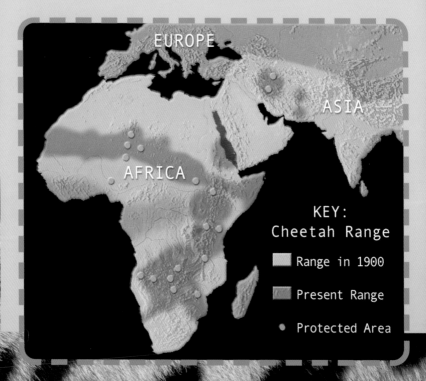

EUROPE

ASIA

AFRICA

KEY:
Cheetah Range

Range in 1900

Present Range

● Protected Area

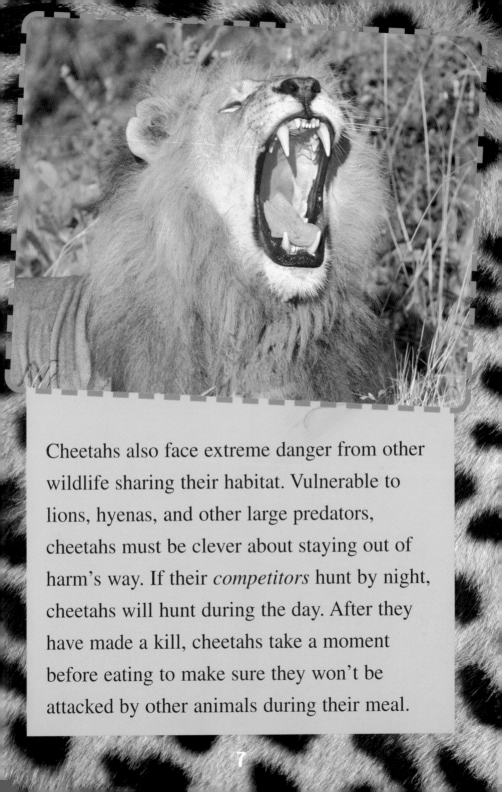

Cheetahs also face extreme danger from other wildlife sharing their habitat. Vulnerable to lions, hyenas, and other large predators, cheetahs must be clever about staying out of harm's way. If their *competitors* hunt by night, cheetahs will hunt during the day. After they have made a kill, cheetahs take a moment before eating to make sure they won't be attacked by other animals during their meal.

Nearly ninety-five percent of cheetah cubs die before they are old enough to reproduce. Sometimes this happens because their mothers are shot, but other times they are simply eaten by hyenas, lions, or birds of prey while their mothers are off hunting. To try to prevent this from happening, a mother cheetah will move her offspring around almost constantly.

Did You Know?

Cheetahs today are all descended from the few animals that survived the Ice Age. Because of this, they are nearly as alike as identical twins.

CHEETAH CHAT

Adult cheetahs have yellowish or tan fur with solid black, round, or oval spots. These spots are fairly small and measure only about 0.75–1.5 inches across. Most of the cheetah's body is covered in spots, except for the white throat and abdomen.

A cheetah's head is small and wedge-shaped, which makes it more *aerodynamic*. The eyes are set high, and the dark "tear" marks under the eyes help reduce the sun's glare – kind of like the dark smudges that professional athletes put under their eyes when they play a game on a sunny day!

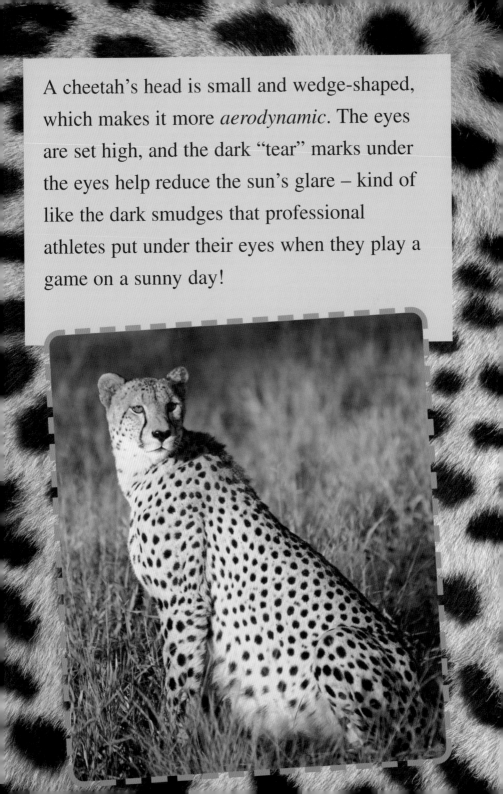

Cheetahs are sometimes mistaken for leopards, but leopards are much heavier cats. Cheetahs are long and lean, and an adult cheetah weighs only 80–140 pounds, stands about 32 inches tall at the shoulder, and ranges from 48 to 56 inches long. Males are slightly larger than females.

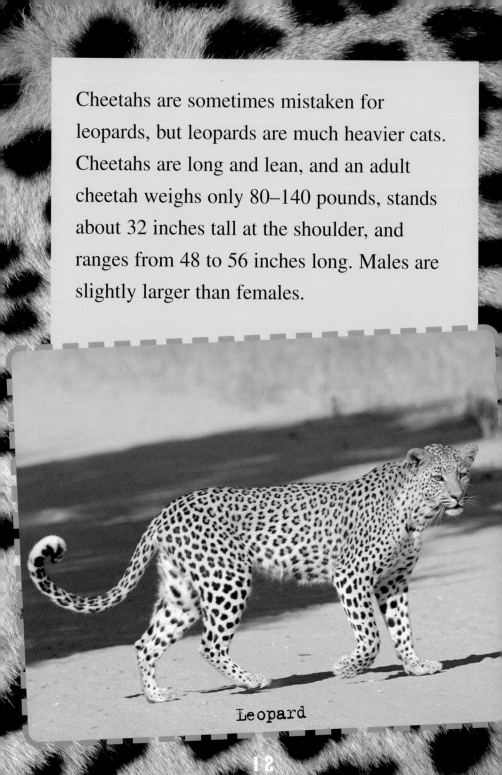

Leopard

Cheetah

Did You Know?

The markings on a cheetah's tail are similar to our fingerprints. Each animal has a distinctive pattern of rings that scientists look for to identify specific animals in the wild.

13

BUILT FOR SPEED

From the special rough pads on the paws, and the *nonretractable* claws for *traction*, to the springlike spine, the cheetah's entire body is built for racing across the grasslands.

The cheetah's long tail acts just like a rudder, helping the cat turn quickly, and its skeleton is light and streamlined. However, even with all of these characteristics, the cheetah can only maintain its maximum speed of almost 70 miles per hour for about 20 seconds.

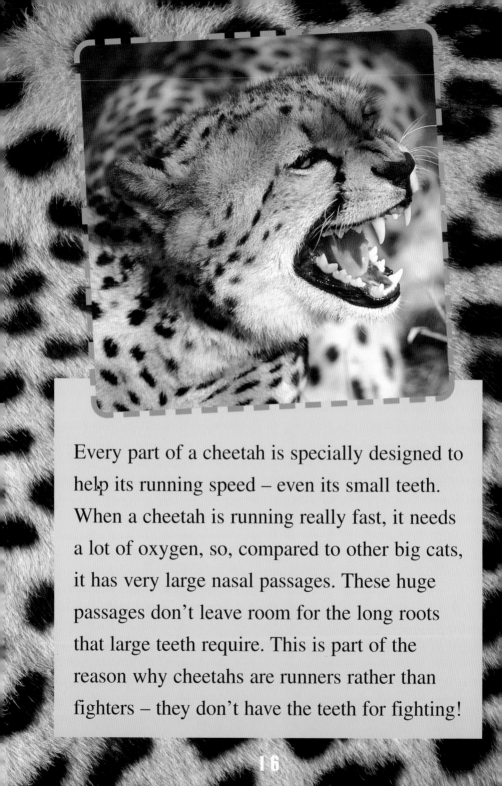

Every part of a cheetah is specially designed to help its running speed – even its small teeth. When a cheetah is running really fast, it needs a lot of oxygen, so, compared to other big cats, it has very large nasal passages. These huge passages don't leave room for the long roots that large teeth require. This is part of the reason why cheetahs are runners rather than fighters – they don't have the teeth for fighting!

When cheetahs communicate, they never roar like the larger species of cats, but they do make many different sounds:

Chirping: a cheetah's chirp sounds kind of like the chirp of a bird or the yelp of a dog. Sometimes their chirps can be heard up to a mile away!

Churring: a fast, high-pitched growl

Nyam-nyam: say it aloud – this is what the cubs sound like when they are feeding

Ihn-ihn: the sound a mother cheetah makes to call her cubs

Purring: a cheetah sounds just like a house cat when it purrs

Staccato purring: when a male cheetah is courting a female, it purrs in very quick, short bursts

Bleating: this sound, which is something like a meow, is a distress call

HELP IN THE WILD

People around the world are beginning to realize that the elegant cheetah could disappear altogether, and are banding together to fight for its survival.

Annie Beckhelling

Annie Beckhelling set up Cheetah Outreach in 1997 after she witnessed the many problems facing wild cheetahs. Cheetah Outreach is run by volunteers and operates from several acres of land that was donated by Spier Wine Estates, in Stellenbosch, South Africa.

Annie wanted to promote the cause of the cheetah by increasing public awareness of the declining number of cheetahs in the wild and, where possible, by breeding cheetahs in captivity. One of the most interesting aspects of the Cheetah Outreach program is the work the volunteers do introducing tame cheetahs to the people of South Africa. Annie believes that people need the opportunity to learn to love and understand cheetahs, so they will work toward saving these beautiful animals.

In Namibia, a country on South Africa's northern border, Cheetah Outreach works in association with the Cheetah Conservation Fund. Recently, Annie visited them to see the work they are doing to help wild cheetahs. On her visit, she helped release a wild cheetah that had been in captivity. She described it as a highlight of her years with these amazing cats.

There are a number of other creative things being done to help cheetahs. Take Merlin, for example. Merlin is an Anatolian shepherd livestock-guarding dog who joined the Cheetah Outreach program in 1998. Merlin acts as an *ambassador* for the Cheetah Conservation Fund's nonlethal predator control program, which teaches farmers how to share their land with wild cheetahs.

Merlin

Originally bred in Turkey to protect herds of goats, sheep, cattle, and even turkeys, the dogs are now being bred in Africa to protect livestock from cheetahs. Instead of trapping and shooting cheetahs, farmers place one of these dogs with their herds as a puppy. The young dogs live, eat, sleep, and travel with the livestock, and instinctively learn to protect the animals from harm.

Over 130 Anatolian shepherds have been placed on Namibian farms. The dogs are not trained to attack. Their job is to bark loudly and stand their ground in order to scare away predators. Cheetahs are not fighting animals by nature, and will run away from a barking dog.

CHEETAHS GO TO SCHOOL

Meet Shadow and Inca. Shadow is a male cheetah who was abandoned by his mother when he was only three days old. He had to be raised by hand. Inca is his half-brother, and was also raised in captivity.

Shadow

Inca

Both cats are ambassadors for Cheetah Outreach. To help save their cousins in the wild, they are taken to South African schools, so that they can educate children about cheetahs.

Because both Shadow and Inca were handraised as cubs, they enjoy interacting with people, especially children. They visit city schools, where children have never had the chance to see a cheetah. All the children can stroke the cheetahs and talk to them.

Educational visits began with Shadow, who enjoys traveling and meeting people. In his first year as an ambassador, Shadow visited more than 50,000 people at schools, clubs, hotels, airports, and even shopping malls.

Five-week-old cheetah cubs

Since then, Cheetah Outreach has grown in more ways than one. In September 1997, Inca became a father when three cubs, Nyana-Spier, Moya, and Charlie, were born at Outreach's breeding center. The births caused great excitement, for cheetahs do not usually breed well in captivity.

Nyana-Spier (which means son of Spier) was the first male born in the litter. He helps Shadow with his community duties and travels to schools and events up and down the country.

In February 2001, Nyana-Spier set a new world speed record. He ran a 100 yard dash in 6.34 seconds. The previous record of 6.60 seconds was held by Moya, his brother.

Nyana-Spier

Moya now lives in the United States, and helps the Angel Fund of Cincinnati with their educational program. The fund raises money to help protect cheetahs in the wild.

WORKING WITH CHEETAHS

An Interview with Katherine Bell

Katherine Bell is a volunteer at Cheetah Outreach. She is a qualified veterinary nurse who came to work for Cheetah Outreach for one month, but loved the cheetahs so much that she stayed on.

Katherine Bell

What is your job at Cheetah Outreach?

When I first joined Outreach, I had to learn all about cheetahs and gain their trust and friendship. Once the cheetahs trusted me,

I could start handling them. Now I care for them, take people into the enclosures to meet them, and answer any questions.

What is working with the cheetahs like?

It's very special. They are wonderful, gentle creatures. Now that they know me, they purr loudly when they see me.

Are you ever scared?

Never. Cheetahs are not aggressive animals. People think that because they are hunters and eat meat they are dangerous. Cheetahs do not attack people, but they must still be treated with respect. We can tell if the cheetahs are upset by looking in their eyes – in just the same way that you can tell when a person is upset. If the cheetahs don't like something or somebody, we quietly move them away so that they are not bothered.

How do you exercise the cheetahs?

Cheetahs are built for speed and it's important that they get plenty of exercise. We have a toy rabbit on a lure, like you see at a greyhound racetrack. The cheetahs chase it around until they are tired. They have lots of fun.

What do you feed the cheetahs?

We feed them chicken, turkey drumsticks, lean red meat, and ostrich liver, stomach, and heart. We try to give them a diet as close as possible to what they'd have in the wild. We do not feed them live prey, as they could hurt themselves chasing the prey in their enclosure.

What do you think the future holds for cheetahs?

Organizations such as Cheetah Outreach and the Cheetah Conservation Fund have achieved a lot in the last few years. One of our biggest achievements has been helping farmers learn to live alongside wild cheetahs. However, there is still a lot to be done if cheetahs are to survive in the wild.

What can we do to help?

You can help us raise funds for cheetah conservation programs. The funds go toward training and placing guard dogs on farms, relocating wild cheetahs in areas where they will be safe, and researching wild cheetah behavior. You can also help by writing stories and articles about cheetahs, reading books, and talking about cheetahs. The more people know about cheetahs, the more people will want to protect this special animal.

We can all work together to change the attitudes and behaviors that endanger cheetahs and help to save them from extinction. We can make a difference!

GLOSSARY

aerodynamic – having a shape that aids fast movement through air

ambassador – representative or messenger

captivity – being held, without freedom to leave. Endangered species are often kept in captivity to live and breed safe from harm.

competitors – animals that hunt the same prey

extinction – when a type or species of animal no longer exists

habitat – the area in which an animal or plant naturally lives

nonretractable – describes claws that cannot be drawn back into the pads of the paws. Unlike the claws of other cats, cheetahs' claws are nonretractable. This provides extra traction.

poaching – the illegal hunting of animals

predators – animals that hunt other animals

traction – grip on a surface

INDEX

CHEETAH WEBSITES

www.cheetah.co.za/

www.cheetahspot.com

www.cheetah.org/Index.html

www.zoobooks.com

www.pbs.org/wnet/nature/cheetahs

If you have enjoyed reading *Cheetah Conservation*, read these other *Storyteller* Chapter Books.

Wolfmaster
Aunt Victoria's Monster
Survival in Cyberspace
A Friend in the Wild
Groovy Gran and the Karaoke Kid
Samantha's Sea
Cat Culture